Rebekah L. Smith

WOOL APPLIQUÉ
folk art

Traditional Projects Inspired by
19th-Century American Life

C&T PUBLISHING

Text copyright © 2015 by Rebekah L. Smith

Photography and artwork copyright © 2015 by C&T Publishing, Inc.

Publisher: Amy Marson

Creative Director: Gailen Runge

Art Director: Kristy Zacharias

Editors: S. Michele Fry and Joanna Burgarino

Technical Editors: Ellen Pahl and Amanda Siegfried

Cover/Book Designer: April Mostek

Production Coordinator: Freesia Pearson Blizard

Production Editor: Katie Van Amburg

Illustrator: Tim Manibusan

Photo Assistant: Mary Peyton Peppo

Style photography by Laura Webb and instructional photography by
Diane Pedersen, unless otherwise noted

Published by C&T Publishing, Inc., P.O. Box 1456, Lafayette, CA 94549

Library of Congress Cataloging-in-Publication Data

Smith, Rebekah L. (Rebekah Leigh), 1971-

 Wool appliqué folk art : traditional projects inspired by 19th-century
American life / Rebekah L. Smith.

  pages cm

 ISBN 978-1-60705-969-1 (soft cover)

1. Appliqué. 2. Folk art--United States. 3. Decorative arts--United
States--History--19th century. 4. Americana. I. Title.

 TT779.S633 2015

 746.44'5--dc23

                            2014036456

Printed in China

10 9 8 7 6 5 4 3 2

CONTENTS

DEDICATION

*For my dedicated husband, Bruce, who never once thought
that writing a book was a crazy idea.*

*Also, to our children, Kelsey, Karly, and Tessa, who have
been as excited as I am about this project.*

ACKNOWLEDGMENTS

So much could be said about the many people who have had a hand in this book, and it would take more than these few words to convey all of the deep gratitude I feel. The Lord has blessed me with a talent I can use. My husband, Bruce, has always supported whatever plans I have pursued. My daughters, Kelsey, who boosts my confidence; Karly, who helped me find my words; and Tessa, my stitching companion, have been the true source of inspiration for this book. My parents, who taught me about all things old and beautiful, have been steadfast in their encouragement.

Friends and family have in so many ways been a part of this book. To Ron and Kathy Wright, who opened up their beautiful home to me to give this book the look I so wanted: thank you. To name everyone who has encouraged me along the way would fill all of this space, but all of you are very important to me. If it's possible, some of you may be even more excited than I am about this book. Thank you. To my new friends at Garth's Auctioneers & Appraisers, Amelia and Kellie, thank you for the use of your photographs of the wonderful antiques you continue to showcase. This book would not be the same without them. Then there are the beautiful styled photographs that were taken by photographer Laura Webb. Thank you for your creativity and patience.

The C&T Publishing family has been a pleasure to work with. When Roxane found me and tossed out the idea of doing a book, I was thrilled to think that someone had such confidence in my work. Thank you, Roxane! So many people have had a hand in this book. Michele and Joanna, my editors, have been with me throughout the writing process and have patiently answered all of my questions and given me direction that was so appreciated. Ellen and Amanda waded through all of the technical information and I cannot thank them enough for their creativity and accuracy. Tim did a great job with all the illustrations and patterns, and I appreciate his attention to detail. April worked tirelessly to get the design of the book to match the feel of the projects. Her artistry was invaluable. My production team of Katie and Freesia kept everything on track and made the book really come together. Diane took subject and instructional photographs that really show my projects in detail.

To all of you who are reading this book and maybe stitching one project or several, I am grateful. Inspiration comes from many places and the support of those you connect with is integral.

INTRODUCTION

Putting together this collection of wool appliqué projects has been challenging and fun. The experience has stretched my creativity and has caused me to take a closer look not only at how I stitch and build a piece of art, but also at how I take it apart. This has allowed me to better understand my work and why I do things a certain way.

When the idea of writing this book began to take shape, I wanted to fill it with a variety of projects. I did not want to write a book of rules. On the contrary, I would like it to be a guide for the beginner and a new challenge for the seasoned stitcher.

In this book, you will find original and exciting wool appliqué patterns and the step-by-step instructions for completing them. As color is an important part of these projects, I have carefully chosen hues and shades that inspire those of us who love the nineteenth-century period and style. The hues have a beauty that I hope you can use and appreciate in your own home.

My true hope is that you enjoy the projects and find your own inspiration in these pages.

WELCOME TO WOOL

If you have never worked with wool before, you may be surprised at the versatility and beauty that can come from this amazing textile. If you *have* worked in wool before, I am sure you know what I am referring to. Wool appliqué is a wonderful textile medium that allows the artist to be creative in a different way from paint or pen. It is all about texture, depth, design, and color. It's also a growing art form, and you can now find many sources for not only inspiration but also materials, which is very important.

Wool will take over your spaces if you are not careful, and it can show up in unexpected closets and cupboards—much to the surprise of your family. Here I will familiarize you with this textile and share my methods for processing wool to obtain a unique look and color. I also include some storage techniques that I have discovered over the years.

I hope this inspires you to think about wool and all of the possibilities for its use.

Piles of hand-dyed wool are ready for use.

Photo by Karly A. Smith

FINDING WOOL

In my wool work I use mostly repurposed wool. I obtain it by going to flea markets, thrift stores, auctions, and yard sales and searching for wool that is really no longer wanted in its current condition but can be processed into something useful. I look for wools that are medium weight, which can be dyed or felted to use in appliqué. These are usually in the form of blankets, skirts, jackets, or even old yardage. Keep an eye out for wools that are plain or only slightly patterned. They are the best to use in appliqué. The other thing to watch for is the color.

The lighter the color, the better it is for dyeing or overdyeing.

When buying wool, avoid wool that is too heavy or too light in weight and wool that is loosely woven, because it will fray.

The other option is to buy wool that is already processed from a wool shop or an individual who sells hand-dyed wools. A growing number of sources are available for those of you who would like to start with wool that is ready to go (see Sources, page 94).

PROCESSING YOUR WOOL

When I use the term *processing*, I am referring to the necessary steps to go from woven wool to felted wool that is ready to use. This usually includes felting and dyeing. I would like to say that I start with a sheep and finish with beautiful woven wool, but that is not the case.

Felting

Felting is the process of getting the wool to be the right texture for an appliqué project. Some wools felt better than others. The wool fibers must bind together. This keeps the edges from fraying and makes the wool very soft and strong. To felt your wool, follow these three simple steps.

1 You need a large cooking pot that you will not use for cooking ever again. I recommend this because the commercial dyes are often acid-based. Put in the wool you want to felt and add water to the pot, covering the wool with at least an inch of water.

2 Bring the water to a boil and let the wool simmer for about 20 minutes. All wool is different, and you will have to see how the differing weaves react when boiled. Let the water cool before removing the wool.

3 Let the wool drip dry. I drape the wool over a clothesline outside in good weather or hang it over my large wash sink in the winter.

This is how I do it, but there are no hard-and-fast rules about felting. You can also throw the wool in the washer and dryer. Both the agitation and heat will felt the woven wool.

Dyeing

I am not a dyeing expert, but I enjoy the process. When I dye wool, I often use natural dyes. If you want to try your hand using commercial dyes, please read and carefully follow the manufacturer's instructions (see Sources, page 94).

Natural dyeing techniques can be a lot of fun as well. My family appreciates that I do this type of dyeing outdoors because of the smell. I have a three-gallon brass kettle that I use for natural dyes as well as felting, and it works wonderfully. I just play around with whatever I can find in my yard or my friends' yards and see what I come up with. I've used black walnuts, goldenrod, and onionskins.

It can be very satisfying to know that you have had more of a hand in your project. Dyeing is certainly not for everyone. I never dreamed that I would take it up, but, well, here we are.

STORING WOOL

Now that you have lots of wool ready to go, you need somewhere to keep it. Trust me, you may start out with just a small pile, but it will grow.

One of my favorite storage options is small plastic bins. The ones I use are clear and roughly 7″ high, 15″ long, and 11″ wide. These are excellent for separating your colors as well as keeping moths out. You can then put the bins in a cupboard, arranged by color, where the wool will be handy and ready for use.

I store bigger wool pieces in a variety of large baskets that I keep in my studio. The baskets are efficient and look nice.

Photo by Karly A. Smith

Plastic bins are a great way to store and sort wool by color.

Lavender keeps the wool moth-free.

> **⟶ hint ⟵**
> *Keep lavender or strong-smelling herbs such as sage with your wool to repel moths.*

My favorite way to store wool scraps is to keep them in clear glass storage jars. I use one- to three-gallon jars. With these also you can separate your colors to have just what you need within easy reach. These look great lined up across a shelf.

Glass jars are perfect for storing wool scraps.

Photo by Karly A. Smith

SNIPPING AND STITCHING

In this section I'll cover the basic steps used to construct the projects in this book. Wool appliqué is really very easy and doesn't require a lot of tools or specific skills. Just select a project, gather the wool in the colors that you have chosen (or vice versa), and you're ready to cut and stitch.

Basic tools you will need for the projects

SUPPLIES FOR CUTTING AND STITCHING

You will need to gather some basic tools and supplies:

- Freezer paper
- Scissors for fabric and paper
- Fine-point felt-tip marker
- Iron
- Pins
- Scissors for thread
- Embroidery needles
- Embroidery floss: DMC #310, #829, #839, #841, #3371*

These are my preferred floss colors.

* These are the floss colors I used in all of the projects in the book: black, dark mustard, medium brown, antique white, and dark brown. They coordinate well with my chosen color palette. Choose floss colors that best complement your own wool colors.

PREPARING THE WOOL PIECES

1 Measure the wool for the background and cut it according to the dimensions given in the Materials list for each project. In general, I add 1″ to the finished width and length measurements to allow for any shrinking that may occur during stitching. The background is trimmed to size later.

2 Trace the pattern pieces onto the dull side of the freezer paper and cut them out on the traced lines. (You may want to make multiples of the same shape, or you can use the same freezer paper pattern several times.)

3 Place the freezer paper pattern pieces onto the appropriate wool, shiny side down. Set your iron for wool, and iron the freezer paper pattern pieces onto the wool. Space them close together for best use of your fabric.

Iron the freezer paper pattern securely to the wool.

4 Cut around the freezer paper pattern attached to the wool, making sure you have all the pieces needed for the project.

5 Keep the wool pieces organized in a plastic bag or multiple bags and set them aside until you are ready to stitch.

6 Lay out all of the wool pieces on the background.

7 Pin only the bottommost layer of wool pieces to the background first. I always stitch the bottom layer to the background first and then add the next layer or layers.

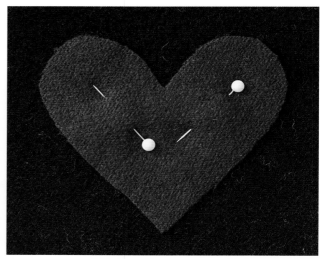

Pin the wool shape to the background.

STITCHING YOUR PROJECT

There are a few basic stitches that are used in all of the projects in this book. Once you have learned these, they can be used in a variety of ways to adhere and embellish your project. I do all of my stitching with two strands of embroidery floss, but you can also use one strand of perle cotton #8. Cut your floss about 18″ long. Longer lengths will tangle and fray as you stitch. I like to use one needle for each floss color as I'm working on a project.

Blanket Stitch

I use the blanket stitch to appliqué wool shapes to a background. Through my teaching, I have learned that each person has a natural rhythm to the stitching and an individual stitch length. I strive for consistent, even stitches, somewhere between ⅛″ and ¼″ long.

1 Knot the end of your floss and bring the needle and floss up through the background, right next to the piece you want to stitch.

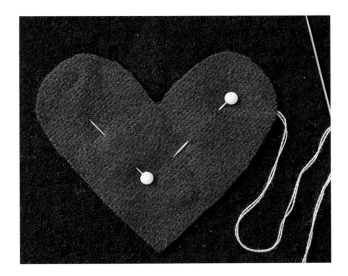

2 Holding the piece you are stitching vertically, insert the needle down through the background 1 stitch length away along the edge of the appliqué. Bring the needle up through the 2 layers 1 stitch length in from the edge.

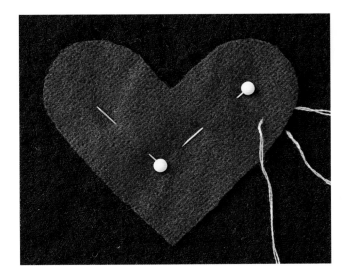

3 Pull the floss through until you have a small loop at the side.

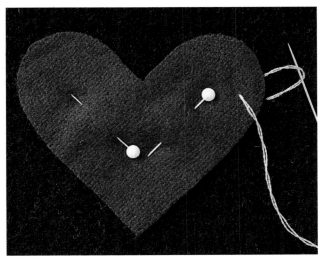

4 Insert the needle through the loop and draw the floss snug against the appliqué piece.

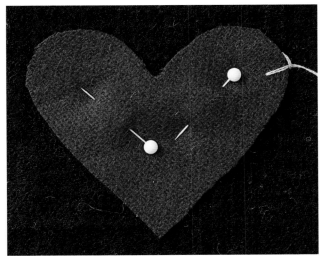

5 Repeat Steps 2–4 all the way around the piece. Repeat Step 1 as needed for any additional pieces and when you need to start a new length of thread.

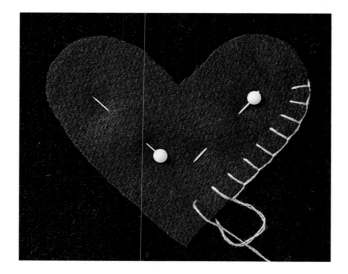

Blanket Stitching Outer Edges

The blanket stitch is also used to finish the raw edges of a wool piece.

1 Knot the floss and come up through the wrong side of your wool, 1 stitch length in from the raw edge. Trim the thread tail close to the knot.

2 Catch a bit of the fabric at the edge as shown, make a loop with your floss, and pull your needle through the loop.

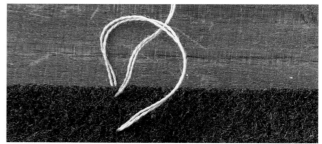

⤙ helpful hints ⤚

When you need to start a new length of floss, stop stitching at the outer edge, after making a stitch into the appliqué. Insert the needle to the wrong side and knot off. Begin stitching inside the previous stitch by bringing your needle up through the background at the right angle. This will hide your stopping and starting points.

To make a crisp corner, insert your needle through the background at the point. Then bring the needle back up again next to where the needle went down to anchor your stitch at the point.

Anchor stitch. ➞

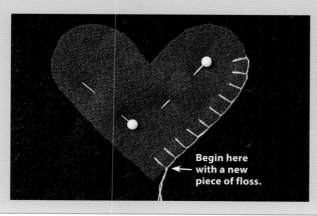

Begin here with a new piece of floss. ⟵

3 Insert the needle into the wool 1 stitch length away and bring the needle up through the loop of thread. Draw it up snugly, but not too tight. Refer to Steps 4 and 5 of Blanket Stitch (pages 15 and 16).

4 To make a crisp corner on the outside, make a tiny stitch at the point and take your needle through the loop to create a knot and anchor your next stitch.

Embroidery Stitches

These stitches are used to add details and decorative elements to the appliqué pieces. I add embroidery stitching last, after the appliqués are stitched to the background. You can stitch them before if you prefer.

OUTLINE STITCH

1 Knot the floss and bring the needle up through the wool at point A. Insert the needle down at B and up at C, about halfway between A and B. Pull the thread through to make a stitch. Insert the needle down again at D and up next to B for the second stitch.

2 Repeat the stitch until you have stitched as far as you want. Keep the stitches even and keep your thread below the line of stitching.

RUNNING STITCH

1 Knot the floss and bring the needle up through the wool. Insert the needle back down to the wrong side and up again to make the stitch.

2 Insert the needle back down and continue to make a series of stitches in a row. Keep the stitch length even and consistent.

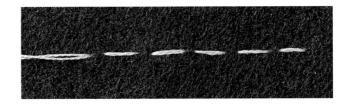

WHIPSTITCH

1 Knot the floss and bring the needle up through the wool. Insert the needle back down to make an angled stitch.

2 Bring the needle up again and continue to make a series of stitches at an angle. These can be close together to close an opening or farther apart to create a design.

FRENCH KNOT

1 Knot the floss and bring the needle up through the wool where you want the French knot. Wrap the floss around the needle 5 times.

2 Push the wraps together and toward the point of the needle.

3 Insert the needle down through the wool, right next to where you came up. Holding on to the wraps with the thumb of your nonsewing hand, pull the needle through to the other side. This will create a round knot on the surface.

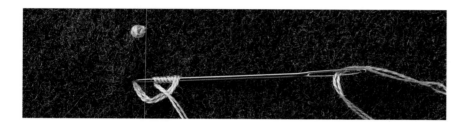

— *hint* —

When I stitch text or other complex designs on light wool, I mark the wool using a fine-point felt-tip marker and stitch with a darker floss. On dark wool, I just wing it. If you want to mark a design on dark fabric, try using a chalk marking pencil in a light color.

STARS

1 Knot the floss and bring the needle up through the wool where you want the center of the star. Insert the needle back down through the wool to make a stitch. This first stitch will determine the size of the star.

2 Repeat the stitch, coming up near the same center hole. Take a stitch in the opposite direction, and then 2 stitches at a 90° angle to make a plus sign (+) or an X.

3 Take a stitch between each of the 4 stitches until you have made a total of 8 to create the star.

FINISHING YOUR PROJECT

You will need a few additional tools to trim and complete your project after stitching the appliqués.

• Rotary cutter* • Cutting mat* • Ruler • Iron with steam setting

* If you don't have a rotary cutter and mat, scissors and painter's tape will work.

1 Set your iron on the wool and steam settings and lay your stitched piece wrong side up on your ironing board. Press the entire piece carefully.

Note: Steam is important to really smooth out the piece.

2 **Using a rotary cutter:** On a cutting mat, measure and trim your piece to the final background dimensions. Make sure the design is centered before trimming.

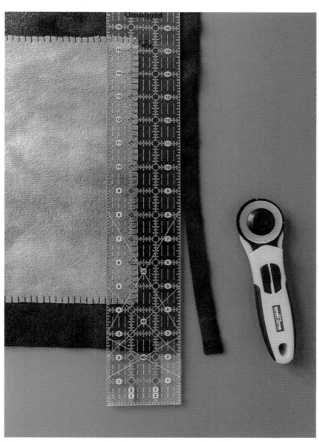

Use a rotary cutter and ruler to cut a straight edge.

Using scissors: Measure each side to the final background dimensions. Use painter's tape to mark each side, making sure the design is centered. Trim the piece with scissors. Pull the tape off carefully so as not to fray the edges of your wool.

Use blue tape and scissors for an alternative trimming method.

After trimming, finish the outer edges with a blanket stitch (see Blanket Stitching Outer Edges, page 16), or use the method described in the project instructions.

Projects

SHADES OF EARTH

Finished Rug: 29″ × 46″ • **Finished Square:** 8½″ × 8½″

W hen contemplating the design of a new piece, inspiration can come from very unexpected places. While visiting a natural history museum, my daughter and I came upon a mat worked by the native peoples of the Northwest Territory. It was worked by hand in different shades of brown sealskin. This beautiful piece was striking for its similarity to the early American textiles with which we are so familiar. I was inspired to work my own version of this mat in wool.

Photo by Garth's Auctioneers & Appraisers, Ohio

Early Native American basket with a woven star motif

I do not always have a clear picture as to how I will use a finished piece, and I find a lot of freedom in this. It makes the creative process fluid and gives it a life of its own. For this rug, I kept adding blocks until the piece felt complete. With that said, inspiration sometimes does come in exact dimensions. You may wish to add more blocks to make the finished rug larger or make fewer blocks to make it smaller.

Color choice is an important component of this rug. My choice to use various shades of brown was a nod to the original as well as the fact that using a simple color palette makes a large piece more versatile in a room setting. Whatever color your choose, this is a good opportunity to use up wool scraps. This is an eye-catching piece for the table, the bed, the back of a couch, or the wall.

This is a great project for using up wool scraps.

MATERIALS

Wool

- 1 medium brown rectangle 30″ × 47″ for background

- 1 brown rectangle 29″ × 46″ for backing

- 8 dark brown squares 9½″ × 9½″ for appliquéd squares

- 15 assorted light to medium dark brown squares 8½″ × 8½″ for large stars

- 15 assorted medium to dark brown squares 6″ × 6″ for medium stars

- 15 light to medium brown squares 4″ × 4″ for circles

- 15 medium to dark brown squares 3½″ × 3½″ for flowers

Other materials

- Embroidery floss: 3 skeins each of antique white, dark brown, and dark mustard

GETTING STARTED

Refer to Preparing the Wool Pieces (page 14) as needed for additional details on these steps.

1 Cut out the wool appliqué pieces using the pattern (pullout page P1).

2 Lay out your appliqués according to the pattern to be sure you have all of the pieces.

SEWING FUN

Refer to Stitching Your Project (page 14) for details on the blanket stitch and embroidery stitches.

1 Stitch a flower, circle, medium star, and large star to each of the 9½˝ squares using the blanket stitch. Add embroidery details.

> **— hint —**
>
> *Be sure to place the large star in the same position on each of the background squares.*

2 Using steam, press each square on the reverse side.

Details of the stitching

3 Trim the squares to 8½″ × 8½″, making sure that the star is centered.

4 Lay out all of the trimmed squares on the 30″ × 47″ wool background rectangle to get the spacing correct. There should be 2¼″ around the edges of the squares along the top, bottom, and sides. Pin the squares securely in place.

5 Blanket stitch the squares to the background.

6 Stitch the remaining stars, circles, and flowers to the background and add embroidery stitching. For these alternate appliqués, I rotated the medium star so that the outer points touch the inner points of the large star. I embroidered a circular design in the center of each flower.

Place squares on background.

Details of stitching

7 Using steam, press the appliquéd piece on the wrong side.

8 Trim the appliquéd top to 29˝ × 46˝. Refer to Finishing Your Project (page 19) as needed.

9 Pin the top and backing fabric together and blanket stitch the outer edges together with 4 strands of floss.

Wow! Congratulations—you've just completed the largest project in the book!

HER LADY'S POCKET

Finished Pocket: Approximately 11½˝ × 14˝

Centuries ago women did not have sewn pockets in their skirts. Instead, they would make themselves a separate "pocket" that would be tied around the waist. These could be as decorative as they were functional. Inspired by these pieces, I designed my own version.

Incorporating some cotton or linen gives a period feel that could not be accomplished using only wool. I chose fabrics with patterns that reflect the eighteenth and nineteenth centuries. Many examples of early pockets were embellished with crewelwork. This influenced my choice to use floral motifs in the design.

Photo by Karly A. Smith

This is a beautiful example of an early lady's pocket.

The pocket incorporates a touch of color and design while still keeping the feel of an earlier, simpler time. One of its more modern functions is to be displayed in the home while serving to store small items. This project could also be worn around the waist, in period tradition.

MATERIALS

Wool

- 1 dark blue rectangle 11″ × 9½″ for background

- 1 blue rectangle 12″ × 4″ for petals and circles

- 1 dark orange rectangle 9″ × 6″ for flower and buds

- 1 light orange rectangle 5″ × 4″ for flower and base

- 1 tan rectangle 5″ × 8″ for accents and circles

Other materials

- ½ yard of cotton print or 2 rectangles 14″ × 16″

- Embroidery floss: 1 skein each of antique white, dark mustard, medium brown, dark brown, and black

- 11″ length of ¾″-wide twill tape

- 2 buttons, ¾″ diameter

- Sewing machine

My wool appliqué version of a pocket

GETTING STARTED

Refer to Preparing the Wool Pieces (page 14) as needed for additional details on these steps.

1 Use the pattern (pullout page P2) to cut out 2 cotton pieces. The pattern includes a ½″ seam allowance.

2 Cut out the wool appliqué pieces and the background using the pattern (pullout page P1). *Note: I did not cut the wool pocket oversized.*

3 Lay out your appliqués according to the pattern to be sure you have all of the pieces.

SEWING FUN

Refer to Stitching Your Project (page 14) for details on the blanket stitch and embroidery stitches.

1 Blanket stitch the appliqués to the wool pocket and add the embroidery.

Details of stitching

2 Position the wool pocket on the right side of the front piece of cotton so that it is 5¼″ down from the top and 1″ up from the bottom. There should be approximately 1⅛″ on each side of the pocket. Pin in place.

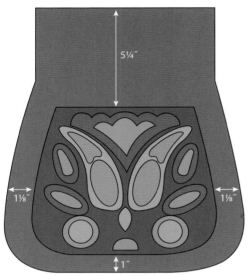

5¼″

1⅛″   1⅛″

1″

Position and pin the pocket in place.

3 Blanket stitch the wool pocket to the cotton, starting at the upper right corner and continuing around the bottom and to the upper left corner. Along the top edge, stitch only the wool layer to create the opening for the pocket.

4 Using steam, press the piece on the wrong side.

5 Pin the 2 pieces of cotton right sides together.

6 Sew the cotton pieces together using a ½″ seam allowance. Leave an opening in the side for turning right side out.

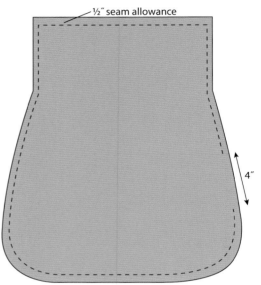

½″ seam allowance

4″

Sew around the edges; leave an opening for turning.

7 Turn the pocket right side out and press.

8 Hand stitch the opening shut with a whipstitch.

9 Cut the length of twill tape into 2 pieces, each 5½″ long. Turn the raw edges under ¼″ and sew the pieces of twill tape to the top of the pocket on the front and back using a whipstitch.

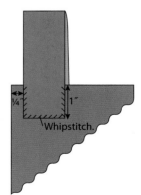

¼″   1″

Whipstitch.

10 Sew the buttons to the twill tape on the front of the piece.

Stitch the twill tape to the cotton backing.

A different cotton print can dramatically change the look of the pocket.

CREATURES OF HABIT

Finished Pillows: 16″ × 12″

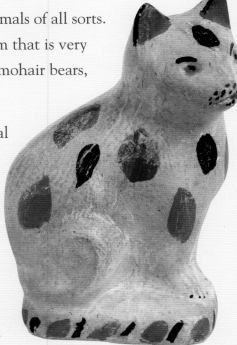

F olk art has a long tradition of interpreting animals of all sorts. They often have a simplified, whimsical charm that is very appealing. Some of my favorites are chalkware cats, mohair bears, and elephant pull toys.

The idea for the cat pillow came from my own special feline, Triss. She sits just that way as she stares out the window watching for birds. In the fall, we have these amazing flocks of blackbirds that come into our yard by the hundreds. Together their many wings make the most incredible sound. As for rabbits, they show up in the most unexpected places. Often I will come upon them on a summer evening as I head from my studio to the house. They keep a watchful eye on me.

This beautiful chalkware cat is a wonderful example of whimsical folk art.

In keeping with my desire to use materials I already have, all of these projects use different fabrics from my shelves. It certainly helps with the budget to be able to use what is in your stash! You can easily adjust the colors to suit your own inspiration and the changing seasons.

Each one of these pillows has its own charm, so make one or all of them and bring a bit of creature comfort into your home.

Photo by Garth's Auctioneers & Appraisers, Ohio

Cat, rabbit, and blackbird can be friends in your home.

MATERIALS

For each pillow

- ½ yard of heavy cotton, twill, or wool fabric, or 2 rectangles 13″ × 17″ for pillow front and back

- 12″ × 16″ pillow form

- Embroidery floss: 1 skein each of antique white, dark brown, and dark mustard

- Sewing machine

Wool for cat

- 1 tan rectangle 14½″ × 11″ for background

- 1 blue rectangle 4″ × 8″ for circles

- 1 dark orange rectangle 3″ × 7″ for hearts and circle

- 1 gray rectangle 5″ × 6″ for cat head and body

- 1 white rectangle 3″ × 5½″ for cat legs

- 1 light orange rectangle 2½″ × 3½″ for spots on cat

- 1 green rectangle 2″ × 12″ for leaves and heart

- 1 tan rectangle 3″ × 3¼″ for flowerpot details

- 1 black rectangle 2½″ × 3″ for flowerpot

Wool for rabbit

- 1 dark brown rectangle 15″ × 11″ for background

- 1 dark mustard rectangle 6″ × 8½″ for rabbit front body

- 1 light mustard rectangle 6″ × 7″ for rabbit hind body

- 1 medium green rectangle 5″ × 9″ for fans

- 1 light green rectangle 4″ × 7″ for smaller fans

- 1 dark green rectangle 3″ × 5″ for fan details

- 1 brown rectangle 1½″ × 12″ for spots

- 1 tan rectangle 1″ × 4″ for ear detail

- 1 white 1½″ square for eye

Wool for blackbird

- 1 light gray rectangle 14″ × 11½″ for the background

- 1 gray rectangle 4″ × 12″ for fence

- 1 dark gray rectangle 4½″ × 6½″ for the bird

- 1 black rectangle 2″ × 3″ for the wings

- 1 light brown rectangle 3″ × 6″ for leaves

- 1 orange rectangle 3″ × 6″ for leaves

- 1 green rectangle 3″ × 6″ for leaves

- 1 mustard rectangle 2″ × 4″ for leaves

- 1 dark brown square 3″ × 3″ for leaf

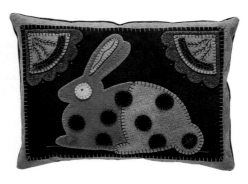

GETTING STARTED

Refer to Preparing the Wool Pieces (page 14) as needed for additional details on these steps.

1 Cut out the wool appliqué pieces using the pattern for the cat, rabbit, or bird (pullout pages P1 or P4).

2 Lay out your appliqués according to the pattern to be sure you have all of the pieces.

SEWING FUN

Refer to Stitching Your Project (page 14) for details on the blanket stitch and embroidery stitches.

1 Blanket stitch the design to the wool background. Add the embroidery details as shown on the patterns.

2 Using steam, press the design on the wrong side. Trim the wool, referring to Finishing Your Project (page 19), as needed. For the cat, trim the background to 13⅛″ × 9¾″. For the rabbit, trim to 13½″ × 9¼″. For the blackbird, trim to 12¾″ × 10″.

3 Center and pin the appliquéd wool rectangle to the right side of the 17″ × 13″ piece of cotton, twill, or wool.

4 Blanket stitch the appliquéd rectangle to the pillow fabric.

5 Pin the pillow rectangle right sides together with the second 17″ × 13″ piece of fabric.

6 Machine sew around the edges using a ¼″ seam allowance and leaving an opening (approximately 12″) along the bottom for turning and inserting the pillow

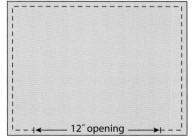

Stitch around the edges and leave an opening at the bottom.

form. I like my pillows to be soft with a flatter look. If you like a fuller pillow, feel free to trim the pillow front and back down by ¼″ to ½″ or sew with a larger seam allowance.

> **━ hint ━**
> *Because I like flatter pillows, I usually remove about one-third of the fill from the pillow form before inserting it. For easy insertion, fold the pillow form in half to insert it into the cover.*

7 Turn the piece right side out and insert the pillow form.

8 Pin the opening together and carefully whipstitch (page 17) the opening closed.

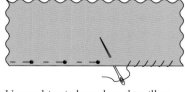

Use a whipstitch to close the pillow.

BIRD OUT OF THE BAG

Finished Bag: 15½″ wide × 14″ high × 5½″ deep

Finished Wool Appliqué: 8½″ × 9½″

I have long been a student of the early folk art that is found here in America—I delight in its wonderful stylized motifs. Flowers and birds are two of the most popular and beautiful of these designs. Birds are a versatile design element. They can be depicted in flight or repose, and there is an endless variety to choose from. I use a lot of birds in my work, with this particular design being inspired by the paintings of the Pennsylvania Germans. These are my roots, and using that as inspiration comes very naturally to me.

What a fabulous example of a bird motif on this antique wallpaper box!

The other element of this project is the bag. Can anyone ever have enough bags? I have always been drawn to the versatile, handled, cloth bag. This project is my idea of how to turn a very plain one into something fun that reflects your style. This tote is an excellent way to transport wool projects as well as a few essentials from the store.

This wool appliquéd bag would be gr
for storing items in an early pant

MATERIALS

Wool

- 1 olive rectangle 9½″ × 10½″ for background

- 1 mustard rectangle 5″ × 7″ for bird

- 1 light blue-green rectangle 4″ × 6″ for flowers and leaves

- 1 dark blue-gray rectangle 3″ × 5″ for flower centers and base

- 1 orange rectangle 2½″ × 3″ for flowers

- 1 brown rectangle 3″ × 5″ for polka dots and wing

- 1 tan square 2″ × 2″ for base detail

Other materials

- 1 jute bag*

- Embroidery floss: 1 skein each of antique white, dark brown, and dark mustard

* See Sources (page 94).

GETTING STARTED

Refer to Preparing the Wool Pieces (page 14) as needed for additional details on these steps.

1 Cut out the wool appliqué pieces using the pattern (pullout page P2).

2 Lay out your appliqués according to the pattern to be sure you have all of the pieces.

SEWING FUN

Refer to Stitching Your Project (page 14) for details on the blanket stitch and embroidery stitches.

1 Blanket stitch the appliqués to the wool background. Embroider the details.

2 Using steam, press your finished piece on the wrong side. Refer to Finishing Your Project (page 19) as needed.

3 Trim to 8½″ × 9½″.

4 Pin the appliquéd wool to the bag and blanket stitch in place.

Details of the stitching

You can never have too many useful and beautiful bags.

WHERE THE HEART IS

Finished Table Rug: 19½″ × 19½″

I have a great affinity for the heart motif. It is timeless and versatile, and I never tire of working it into a design. My inspiration for this particular piece came from antique valentines that were cut out of folded paper and embellished with ink and watercolor. They were often symmetrical and ranged from simple to complex designs. These valentines were usually inscribed with poems or verse. They were given as mementos and are sometimes found tucked away in old books. The heart can be found in all areas of American folk art and is an easy motif to weave into a project.

This early valentine has both hand-painted and hand-cut embellishments.

In this rug I worked in some medium brown velvet for the background. It has a beautiful, soft look and is surprisingly easy to work with. Feel free to replace the velvet with wool if you like. My earth-toned color choices are the result of simply knowing how I wanted the piece to look and feel. Of course, it would be just as wonderful done in reds.

6 Place a tan wool 1″ × 12½″ strip on the background, overlapping the velvet ¼″. Pin along the edge. Add a strip to the opposite side and pin. Repeat to add the tan 1″ × 14½″ strips to the remaining 2 sides. Trim the ends of the strips as needed.

7 Blanket stitch the strips in place.

8 Finish the outer scalloped edge with a blanket stitch and stars.

9 Using steam, press the finished piece on the wrong side. I'm thrilled you chose this project!

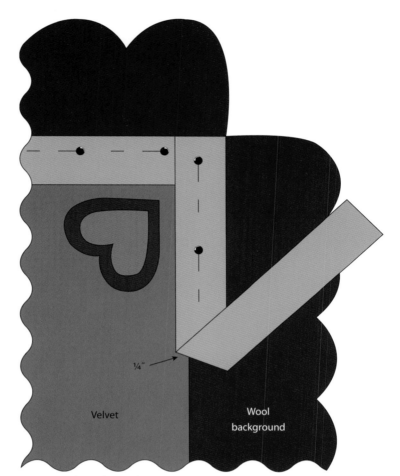

¼″

Velvet

Wool background

Position and pin the wool strips securely.

Detail of stitching in the scalloped background

FOR NEEDLES AND THREAD

Finished Caddy: 12½″ × 8½″

Sewing caddies have long been used by both men and women to carry or store the implements necessary for repairing garments. While some were roll-ups for travel, others were decorative as well as useful, made to hang on the wall, like this project. Others were actual wooden boxes with drawers and spool holders. There were also pincushions shaped like birds, shoes, flowers, and so on.

This beautifully crafted antique sewing box was versatile and useful.

Photo by Garth's Auctioneers & Appraisers, Ohio

Before the sewing machine, hand stitching was the only option, and having the proper tools handy was essential. Clothing, bedding, and linens were constantly being mended and reused.

Here again I've used both cottons and wool. This project combines my love of color and design to brighten up my decor with the desire to make something useful as well. Hang this in a sewing room or studio to keep sewing notions handy. Mixing a patterned background fabric with an intricate wool design will give your piece that period feel. There was a time when people used every scrap of material they had and invented interesting, beautiful designs because of it.

The sewing caddy was an important part of the household and was kept handy in case of need.

MATERIALS

Cotton

- 1 rectangle 10″ × 14″ or
  1 fat quarter* for backing

- 1 rectangle 10″ × 14″ for front

- 1 rectangle 4″ × 10″ for pocket

- 1 strip 2″ × 30″ for
  binding straight edges

- 1 strip 2″ × 13″ cut on the
  bias for binding curved edge

Wool

- 1 red rectangle 4″ × 10″
  for heart and flower

- 1 tan square 5″ × 5″ for flower

- 1 mustard rectangle 3″ × 5″
  for design on heart

- 1 green rectangle
  4″ × 6″ for leaves

- 1 light green rectangle
  1¼″ × 5″ for circles

Other materials

- 1 rectangle 10″ × 14″
  of thin batting

- 5½″ length of ¾″-wide twill tape

- Embroidery floss: 1 skein
  each of antique white, dark
  brown, and dark mustard

- Scraps of batting or wool
  fleece for stuffing

* A fat quarter measures 18″ × approximately 21″.

GETTING STARTED

Refer to Preparing the Wool Pieces (page 14) as needed for additional
details on these steps.

1 Cut the background, backing, and pocket from the cotton using the
patterns (pullout page P4). Use the background pattern to cut the batting.

2 Cut out the wool appliqué pieces using the patterns.

3 Lay out your appliqués according to the pattern to be sure you have all
of the pieces.

4 Turn the fabric under ¼″ to the wrong side all the way around the
pocket piece and press with an iron.

SEWING FUN

Refer to Stitching Your Project (page 14) for details on the blanket stitch, whipstitch, and embroidery stitches.

1 With embroidery floss, use a running stitch to loosely gather the top of the pocket until it is about 4½″ wide. Secure it with a knot.

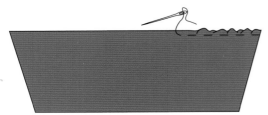

Gather the pocket.

2 Center and pin the pocket securely to the cotton background 1″ from the bottom. Stitch around the pocket using a blanket stitch and leaving the top open.

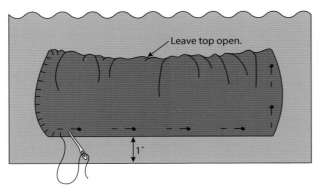

Pin and stitch the pocket to the background.

3 Blanket stitch the wool pieces to the front, above the pocket, but leave an opening along the edge of the red flower and heart for inserting the stuffing. Embroider the details.

4 Stuff the heart and flower with a small amount of batting or fleece. Finish the blanket stitching to close the opening.

Details of the stitching

5 Using steam, press the piece on the wrong side.

6 Layer the front, batting, and backing pieces together, with the batting in the middle and right sides of the front and backing facing out. Pin together.

7 Fold the long edges of the binding strips over to the wrong side ¼″ and press. Then fold the binding in half with wrong sides together and press again.

8 Open the bias binding and pin it to the curved edge along the front and backing. Trim the length as needed. Repeat for the bottom and sides with the remaining binding strip, turning the raw edges of the side strips under ¼″. Stitch the front and then the back of the binding using a blanket stitch.

9 Center and pin the twill tape along the top of the backing, turning the raw edges under ¼″. Sew with a whipstitch as shown.

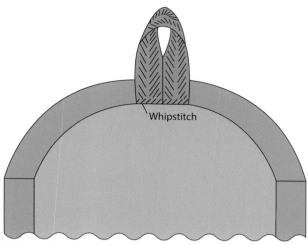

Whipstitch the twill tape to the backing.

The sewing caddy is useful as well as decorative.

WOOLY WINDOW

Finished Table Rug: 46″ × 13¾″

I n drawing inspiration for my pieces, I often turn to antique quilts for their comfortable elegance and functional beauty. Whether they are pieced quilts or appliquéd, there is much to be gained by studying their designs. Often they were the original work of the maker, who may have been inspired by her surroundings, or they were a pattern reflecting the popular trends of that time. Quilts have never gone out of style and continue to give us joy and warmth.

Album quilts, such as this early example, are a marvel of creativity.

This table rug is my interpretation of the many floral motifs used by those early quilters. I am constantly drawn to the bold, simple designs of flowers and leaves, and I use them in my patterns, finding new joy each time. The colors I used here give the piece a fresh look, while keeping it warm with just a touch of color. I'm sure you've noticed my affinity for brown and earthy tones. They are a versatile group and an endless palette from which to draw. Here again I have used a textile in addition to the wool. I used linen for the base of the wool appliqués, although wool will work just as well. The linen lightens the piece up and lends an early feel through its woven texture.

This was a very satisfying piece and can be used in many ways. It hangs over the railing in my stairway and I look at it first thing every day. Enjoy stitching!

This table rug is well placed atop an old-surfaced farm table.

MATERIALS

Wool

- 1 rectangle 40″ × 13¾″ for backing

- 1 dark brown rectangle 12½″ × 25″ for appliqué background

- 1 medium brown rectangle 12½″ × 12½″ for appliqué background

- 1 dark green rectangle 8″ × 15″ for leaves

- 1 light green rectangle 10″ × 14″ for leaves

- 1 dark brown rectangle 6″ × 10″ for flowers and bud accent

- 1 mustard rectangle 4″ × 5″ for flower centers and bud

- 1 orange rectangle 6″ × 8″ for flower and bud

- 1 dark red square 3″ × 3″ for flower

- 1 blue rectangle 1½″ × 11″ for berries

- 1 brown rectangle 4″ × 30″ for tongues

- 1 tan rectangle 4″ × 20″ for tongues

Other materials

- 1 linen rectangle 42″ × 16″ for background

- Embroidery floss: 3 skeins of dark mustard, 2 skeins of antique white, and 1 skein of dark brown

GETTING STARTED

Refer to Preparing the Wool Pieces (page 14) as needed for additional details on these steps.

1 Cut out the wool appliqué pieces for Panels A, B, and C and the wool for the tongues using the patterns (pullout pages P2 and P3).

2 Lay out the appliqués for each panel to be sure you have all of the pieces.

3 Cut the dark brown 12½″ × 25″ rectangle in half to make 2 squares 12½″ × 12½″.

SEWING FUN

Refer to Stitching Your Project (page 14) for details on the blanket stitch and embroidery stitches.

1 Stitch the appliqués for Panels A and C to the dark brown squares and stitch the appliqués for Panel B to the medium brown square. Add the embroidery details.

2 Using steam, press each piece on the wrong side and trim to 11½″ × 11½″. Refer to Finishing Your Project (page 19), as needed.

3 Pin and stitch the squares to the linen, leaving 1¼″ in between each and centering them across the 16″ width.

4 Using steam, press the piece on the wrong side.

5 Trim the linen to 41″ × 14¾″.

6 Stitch the smaller tan tongues to the brown tongues and blanket stitch the outer curved edges. Press using steam.

7 Turn the linen under ½″ on all sides and press using steam.

8 Pin the finished top to the wool backing, leaving the short ends open.

9 Line up 5 tongues on each short end, placing the flat sides between the linen and wool backing. Allow about 3″ of the tongues to extend beyond the edge of the linen and wool backing. Pin the tongues in place.

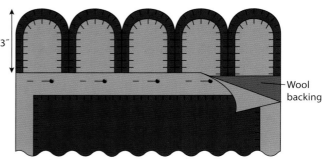

Arrange tongues and pin in place.

10 Blanket stitch the outer edges all the way around the piece. Stitch on both the front and the back of the short ends to secure the tongues. You'll stitch through the linen and tongues on the front, and through the backing and tongues on the back.

11 Press once more, using steam, and you have a new treasure!

Panel A

Panel B

Panel C

WOOLY BINDINGS

Finished Book: 8″ × 8½″ (closed) • 16″ × 8½″ (open)

B ooks, old and new, have held a fascination for me as long as I can recall. I enjoy what is housed inside their pages, but their exteriors can be inspiring as well. I can never have enough old books: from the oldest leather-bound books that were individually sewn together, to the decorative covers expertly tooled with intricate designs, and even to the illustrated covers of the early twentieth century. That leads me to the other kinds of books in my collection—the books of my trade. Journals, sketchbooks, and sewing books are all very necessary to the textile artisan.

These lovely old books have a beauty all their own.

This particular book is another version of what I consider a sewing caddy. It is that important organizer of needle, thread, and scissors. It keeps my work on track and is handy to travel with. Inside is a needle flap, a pincushion, and a pocket. My sewing caddy has been to countless school events, waiting rooms, guild meetings, car rides, campgrounds, hotel rooms, and the list goes on and on.

It is also a conversation piece; the curious are always looking for a glimpse inside. Some are surprised by what they find, and others want to know where they can get one.

This is another opportunity to use scraps of wool and cotton that have been accumulating. I save any leftover piece of fabric that may be large enough to work into another project.

This book of sewing projects looks right at home with vintage sewing items.

MATERIALS

Wool

- 2 dark brown rectangles 8½″ × 9½″ for front and back covers

- 2 assorted rectangles 8½″ × 9½″ for interior

- 1 off-white rectangle 6½″ × 7½″ for arched panel

- 1 red rectangle 4″ × 6″ for front cover flower and embroidered base

- 1 dark green rectangle 5½″ × 7″ for needle flap

- 1 dark blue rectangle 3″ × 7″ for flower basket

- 1 dark green square 5″ × 5″ for large interior flower

- 1 mustard rectangle 4″ × 5″ for front cover oval and interior flower

- 1 blue square 5″ × 5″ for front cover triangle and interior flower center

- Assorted wool scraps for leaves

Other materials

- 2 cotton strips 2½″ × 9″ for binding

- Batting scraps or wool fleece

- 2 pieces 8″ × 7″ of chipboard

Front and back cover of the book

Interior of the book

GETTING STARTED

Refer to Preparing the Wool Pieces (page 14) as needed for additional details on these steps.

1 Cut out the wool appliqué pieces using the patterns (pages 65–67).

2 Lay out your appliqués according to the pattern to be sure you have all of the pieces.

SEWING FUN

Refer to Stitching Your Project (page 14) for details on the blanket stitch and embroidery stitches.

Front Cover

1 Pin the arched panel to the dark brown 8½″ × 9½″ background, 1¼″ from the top, right, and bottom and 1¾″ from the left side.

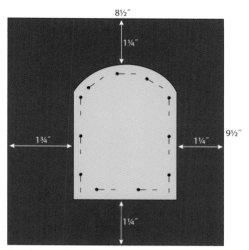

Pin the panel in place.

2 Blanket stitch the panel to the background.

3 Stitch the remaining front cover appliqué pieces to the panel background and embroider the details.

4 Using steam, press the piece on the wrong side.

5 Trim ½″ off each side so that the piece measures 7½″ wide and 8½″ long. Refer to Finishing Your Project (page 19). *Note: The panel should be offset to the right to allow for the binding.*

Back Cover

1 Blanket stitch the 2 layered leaves to the remaining dark brown background. Embroider the details.

2 Using steam, press the piece on the wrong side.

3 Trim ½″ off each side so that the piece measures 7½″ wide and 8½″ long.

Left Interior

1 Blanket stitch 3 layered leaves to the needle flap. Embroider the details.

2 Using steam, press the needle flap on the wrong side.

3 Pin the needle flap to an 8½″ × 9½″ background rectangle, 1½″ from the top and 1¼″ from the left side.

4 Blanket stitch the needle flap to the background along the top edge only.

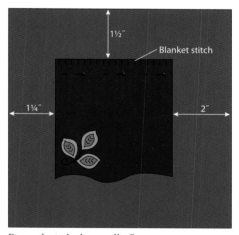

Pin and stitch the needle flap.

5 Continue the stitching around the needle flap only.

6 Using steam, press from the wrong side. Trim ½″ from all sides so that the piece measures 7½″ wide and 8½″ long. *Note: The needle flap should be offset to the left to allow for the binding.*

Right Interior

1 Pin the basket to the remaining 8½″ × 9½″ background rectangle, 1¼″ up from the bottom and 1″ from the right side. Blanket stitch the basket in place along the sides and bottom. Along the top, stitch only the basket, leaving the top open.

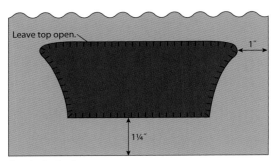

Stitch the basket.

2 Stitch the flowers and leaves to the background.

3 Stitch the circle to the flower center until you have a 1″ opening.

4 Put a little batting or wool fleece in the circle and finish the stitching.

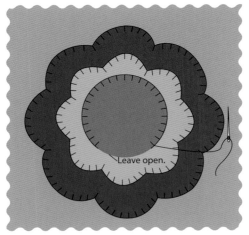

Stuff the flower center.

5 Finish by embroidering the details.

6 Using steam, press from the wrong side. Trim ½″ from all sides so that the piece measures 7½″ wide and 8½″ long.

Binding

1 Press the edges of the 2½″ × 9″ cotton strips under ¼″ to the wrong side.

2 Arrange the front cover and back cover right side up, aligning the top and bottom edges and leaving 1″ in between them.

3 Place a cotton strip on top of the 2 pieces, overlapping ½″ on each side. Pin in place and blanket stitch the edges to the wool.

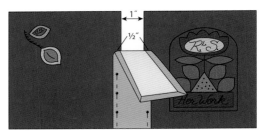

Pin and stitch a cotton strip to the front and back cover.

4 Repeat Step 3 for the interior pieces, with the needle flap on the left and the flower on the right.

5 Using steam, press both pieces on the wrong side.

6 Pin the front and back together with right sides out.

7 Start at the bottom of the right side and stitch the front and back together along the sides and top; leave the bottom open.

8 Slide a piece of chipboard into the opening along the bottom, one on each side of the binding.

9 Stitch the bottom closed.

10 Stitch up the center of the cotton binding strips using a whipstitch in one direction. Stitch again in the opposite direction to create a cross-stitch.

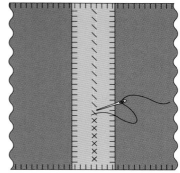

Cross-stitch the binding.

Detail of stitching the cotton binding

— hint —

When beginning the blanket stitch along the outer edges of the cotton binding, insert your needle between the binding and the wool to hide the knot at the end of your floss.

FLOWERS FOR THE TABLE

Finished Table Rug: 20½˝ × 14½˝

A *fraktur*'s charm is often in its imperfection such as in this early example.

W hen searching for inspiration, I have looked often to the objects used by immigrants who came to this country hundreds of years ago. They brought with them their own traditions and regional folk art. The German *fraktur* is an example of the beauty that can be found in the inspired but untrained hand of one who is looking for color and beauty to add to their surroundings. These pen and watercolor documents were originally used as baptismal, birth, and marriage commemorative pieces, but they also include bookplates and certificates given to students. They comprise commonly used motifs such as tulips, birds, urns, houses, people, and more.

I have chosen the tulip for this table rug, as it is another of my favorite subjects. Although the early *frakturs* were colorful in their origins, I have chosen a muted palette as if this piece had been lovingly put on display and has since aged to a soft patina. With the idea in mind to use this on a table, I inverted the center tulip so that the observer could admire it from any vantage point. Once again I have combined a linen background with the wool. The linen gives the feel of the early handmade paper used in the creation of a *fraktur*. These items are a connection to historic traditions; stitching this textile version can give you a glimpse into that past.

How about these flowers for the center of your kitchen table?

MATERIALS

Wool

- 1 rectangle 18″ × 12″ for backing

- 1 medium brown wool rectangle 7″ × 12″ for center appliqué background

- 1 off-white wool rectangle 6″ × 10″ for tulips

- 1 light green wool rectangle 5½″ × 17″ for stems and leaves

- 1 black wool rectangle 6″ × 8″ for tulip accents, 6 circles, and 1 flowerpot

- 1 medium brown wool rectangle 4½″ × 10½″ for 3 circles and
  2 flowerpots

- 1 tan wool rectangle 2½″ × 4″ for tulip accents

- 1 dark green wool rectangle 2″ × 10″ for leaf accents

- 2 black wool strips 2¼″ × 31″ for scalloped border

- 20 assorted brown and tan scraps 1½″ × 2½″ for scallops

Other materials

- 1 linen rectangle 18½″ × 12½″ for background

- Embroidery floss: 1 skein each of antique white, dark mustard,
  and dark brown

> **⟶ hint ⟶**
>
> *This table rug is an excellent opportunity to use up those wool*
> *scraps that you've been collecting. You can include 20 scraps for*
> *the scallops in the border.*

GETTING STARTED

Refer to Preparing the Wool Pieces (page 14) as needed for additional details on these steps.

1 Cut out the wool appliqué pieces using the patterns (pullout page P1).

2 Lay out your appliqués according to the pattern to be sure you have all of the pieces.

3 Cut each of the black wool 2¼″ × 31″ strips into 1 strip 2¼″ × 12″ and 1 strip 2¼″ × 18″.

4 Trace the scallop border pattern (pullout page P1) onto freezer paper 4 times for the short borders and 6 times for the long border.

5 Cut out and press the freezer paper to the black wool strips. Cut along the scalloped edge to make the borders.

Cut the scalloped borders.

Sewing Fun

Refer to Stitching Your Project (page 14) for details on the blanket stitch and embroidery stitches.

1 Blanket stitch the appliqués for one flower to the 7″ × 12″ brown background. Embroider the details.

Details of the stitching

2 Using steam, press the finished rectangle on the wrong side and trim to 6″ × 11¼″. Refer to Finishing Your Project (page 19).

3 Pin the piece to the center of the linen so that it is 6¼″ from the sides of the linen background and centered from top to bottom. Blanket stitch to the linen.

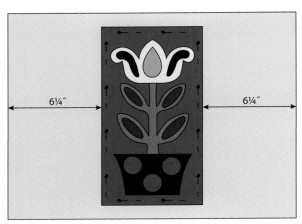

Appliqué placement guide

> — **hint** —
>
> *To give your rug an authentic look, use different colors of floss as I did. It reminds me of a time when people made do with what they had on hand. It's all about the details.*

4 Blanket stitch a tulip to the linen on both sides of the rectangle. The flower should be about ¼″ away from the brown wool center rectangle. Add the embroidery stitches.

5 Using steam, press the finished piece on the wrong side.

6 Turn under a ¼˝ hem on all sides of the linen and press.

7 Blanket stitch the scallops to the black scalloped border strips by positioning the curved edge of each scallop ¼˝ from the curved edge of the border. Pin in place and blanket stitch the curved edges only. The straight edge will be layered between the linen top and the wool backing. Press each border strip, using steam, on the wrong side.

8 Layer the wool backing and the linen top with wrong sides together. Insert the finished borders between the backing and the top so that ¾˝ of the border is between the layers. Pin the layers together.

9 Blanket stitch around all of the straight edges on both sides. Stitch through the border and linen on the front, and through the border and wool backing on the back. Then blanket stitch the outer scalloped edges.

Stitch scallops to the border strips.

HOUSING FOR PAPERS

Finished Hanging Bag: 17″ × 22″

The house is a much-used decorative motif, here painted on an early apple box.

Photo by Garth's Auctioneers & Appraisers, Ohio

This hanging bag resulted from a combination of necessity and the desire to make something decorative. We have an old house with a limited amount of space for storage. I was looking for a way to store my current reading material without having it lying on a stand or in a pile. By now you may have realized that I have a fondness for bags of all sorts. I designed this bag based on old grain bags that were woven of heavy cotton or linen and used over and over for hauling and storing seed and feed. They are homely relics of a time when one reused or repurposed everything. I collect these old bags and sometimes incorporate them into my work if they are in poor condition and not suitable for preserving.

The design incorporated onto this bag reflects my love of old houses. They constantly give me ideas to use in my work and are an endless source of enthusiasm. Having an old house of my own, I cannot help but have a great affection for these early structures that have stood through time and give us a sense of history.

I searched for fabrics that resemble early textiles to use in this hanging bag. Store papers and periodicals to keep handy for those moments when you want to spark creativity. Hang the bag by a chair, bed, or any place where it will find a purpose.

You'll want to keep this piece handy for stashing your reading material.

MATERIALS

Wool

- 1 blue wool rectangle 10″ × 12″ for appliqué background

- 1 blue wool rectangle 5″ × 11″ for arch

- 1 dark orange wool rectangle 5″ × 10″ for smaller arch, sun, and chimney

- 1 mustard wool rectangle 6″ × 7″ for darker leaves and tree

- 1 green wool rectangle 6″ × 7″ for lighter leaves and tree

- 1 light tan wool square 3½″ × 3½″ for house

- 1 medium tan wool rectangle 3½″ × 5″ for house (gable end)

- 1 gray wool rectangle 2″ × 5″ for roof

- 1 brown wool square 3″ × 3″ for door and tree trunk

- 1 light orange wool rectangle 2″ × 3″ for inner sun detail

- 1 black wool rectangle 1½″ × 3″ for windows

Other materials

- ¾ yard of heavy cotton or linen for backing

- ½ yard of heavy cotton or linen in contrasting color for pocket

- Embroidery floss: 2 skeins of dark mustard and 1 skein each of antique white, medium brown, and dark brown

- ⅓ yard (12″) of ¾″-wide twill tape

- 2 buttons, ¾″ diameter

- Sewing machine

GETTING STARTED

Refer to Preparing the Wool Pieces (page 14) as needed for additional details on these steps.

1 Cut out the wool appliqué pieces using the arch pattern (pullout page P3) and the remaining patterns (pages 80 and 81).

2 Cut 2 rectangles 18″ × 23″ from the heavy cotton or linen for the backing.

3 Cut 1 rectangle 14½″ × 15″ from the heavy cotton or linen for the pocket.

4 Lay out your appliqués according to the pattern to be sure you have all of the pieces.

SEWING FUN

Refer to Stitching Your Project (page 14) for details on the blanket stitch and embroidery stitches.

1 Blanket stitch the house, tree, and sun appliqués to the 12″ × 10″ blue wool background. Stitch the small arch to the larger one. Embroider the details.

2 Using steam, iron the blue wool appliquéd piece on the wrong side. Trim to 11″ × 9″. Refer to Finishing Your Project (page 19) as needed.

3 Place the 18″ × 23″ cotton or linen backing pieces right sides together and sew by machine using a ½″ seam allowance and leaving an opening on one side.

4 Turn the backing right side out, press with an iron, and hand-stitch the opening shut using a whipstitch (page 17).

Details of the stitching

5 Turn under the edges of the pocket ¼″ on all sides and press. Sew the hem around the edges by machine. The pocket will measure 14½″ wide and 14″ long.

6 Center and pin the blue wool appliquéd piece on the pocket fabric, approximately 2½″ down from the top 14½″ edge. Blanket stitch in place.

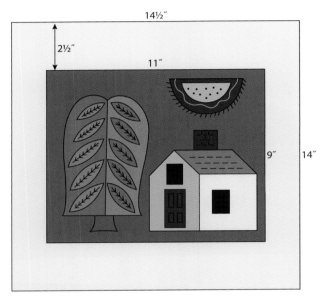

Stitch appliqué to pocket.

7 Center and pin the pocket to the backing fabric, approximately 6½″ down from the top. Blanket stitch in place, starting on the right side and leaving the top open.

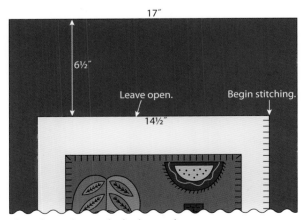

Place the pocket on the background.

8 Stitch along the top of the pocket fabric only.

9 Pin the arch to the backing fabric, 1½″ down from the top and centered from side to side. Blanket stitch in place.

10 Cut 2 pieces of twill tape 5″ long and turn the cut ends under ¼″.

11 Pin each piece 1″ from the side of the backing and 1″ down from the top. Sew to the front and to the back using the blanket stitch.

12 On the front, sew a button onto each loop of twill tape.

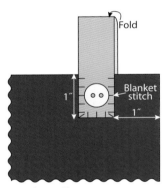

Sew the twill tape.

The hanging bag in alternate colors is both useful and decorative.

Outline stitch

Outline stitch

TULIP HARMONY

Finished Table Rug: 35″ × 11¾″

I have spent a great deal of time studying the early dower chest, also called a blanket box. These large wooden boxes were used for storage of items including blankets, sheets, quilts, clothing, and many other household items. Some of them were highly deco-

Early Pennsylvania German blanket boxes such as this one were often highly decorated.

Photo by Garth's Auctioneers & Appraisers, Ohio

rated while others simply bore the owner's initials and a date. They are found in many regions of the eastern and midwestern United States and were painted with motifs such as tulips, birds, unicorns, urns, eagles, and pinwheels to name just a few. These were well crafted and important pieces of furniture and are now highly sought after works of folk art.

What I like about the design of this table rug is the symmetry, and the mixture of folk art motifs with a very geometric pattern. The tulips lie on an arched panel that mirrors the panels often found on an early blanket box. The tulip panels give definition to the ends of the piece and allow it to be used on a table. An item placed in the center won't cover up the focal point of the design. It would also be striking as a wallhanging.

This table rug belongs on a bureau, cedar chest, or any number of places, fitting well in a nineteenth-, twentieth-, or even twenty-first-century home. It will add a sense of warmth and design to any interior.

MATERIALS

Wool

- 1 dark brown rectangle 34″ × 12¾″ for background

- 1 brown rectangle 33″ × 11¾″ for backing

- 1 tan rectangle 8″ × 32″ for arched panels, squares, and circles

- 1 dark orange rectangle 4″ × 20″ for squares

- 1 orange rectangle 4″ × 20″ for circles

- 1 brown rectangle 5″ × 11″ for circles

- 1 green rectangle 10″ × 12″ for leaves

- 1 light green rectangle 7″ × 8″ for leaves

- 1 medium brown rectangle 3″ × 8″ for tulips

- 1 dark orange rectangle 3½″ × 6″ for tulip accents and circles

- 1 dark brown rectangle 4″ × 6″ for urns

- 1 light brown rectangle 2″ × 4½″ for urn accents

- 1 dark green rectangle 4″ × 12″ for sawtooth borders

Other materials

- Embroidery floss: 2 skeins of dark mustard and 1 each of antique white and dark brown

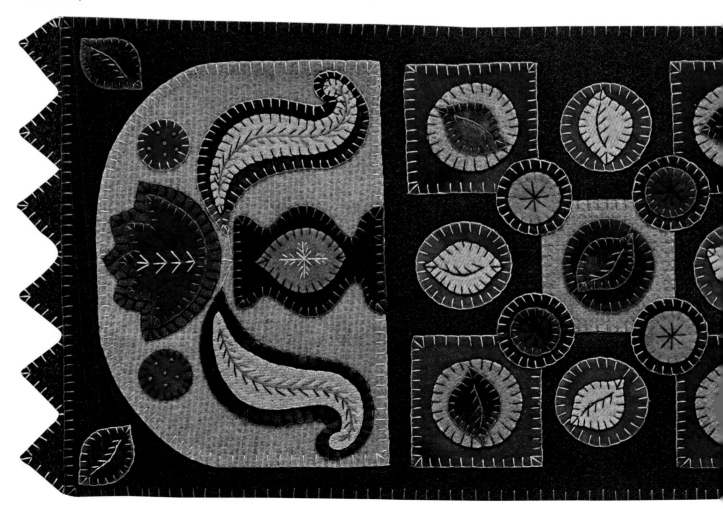

GETTING STARTED

Refer to Preparing the Wool Pieces
(page 14) as needed for additional details
on these steps.

1 Cut out the wool appliqué pieces using
the patterns (pullout page P3).

2 Lay out your appliqués according to the
pattern to be sure you have all of the pieces.

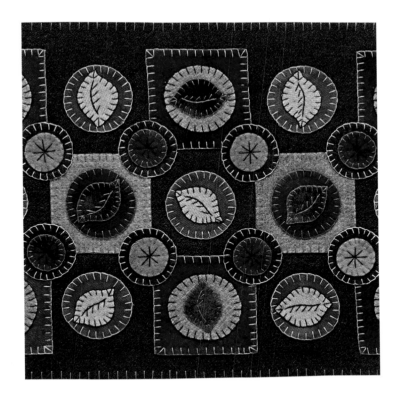

SEWING FUN

Refer to Stitching Your Project (page 14) for details on the blanket stitch and embroidery stitches.

1 Pin the tan arched panels to each end of the background pieces, placing each arch 1¼˝ from the end.

2 Blanket stitch the arches to the backing.

3 Stitch the urn, leaves, tulip, and circles to the panel. Add embroidery details.

4 Lay out all of the squares on the background and pin, leaving ½˝ between the first row of squares and the bottom of each arched panel.

Carefully space the squares before stitching.

Details of stitching

5 Stitch the squares to the background.

6 Lay out and pin the 7 orange 2¼˝ circles between the squares, making sure they are centered.

7 Stitch the circles to the background.

8 Stitch the remaining circles and leaves. Embroider the details.

9 Stitch and embroider the leaves in the corners.

10 Using steam, press the entire finished piece on the wrong side.

11 Trim the finished piece to 33˝ × 11¾˝. Refer to Finishing Your Project (page 19) as needed.

12 Blanket stitch the outer edges of both sawtooth borders.

13 Pin the sawtooth borders between the finished piece and the backing.

14 Blanket stitch around the entire piece, stitching both the front and the back of the sawtooth borders.

15 Using steam, press the entire finished piece.

Blanket stitch the edges.

Details of the squares and circles

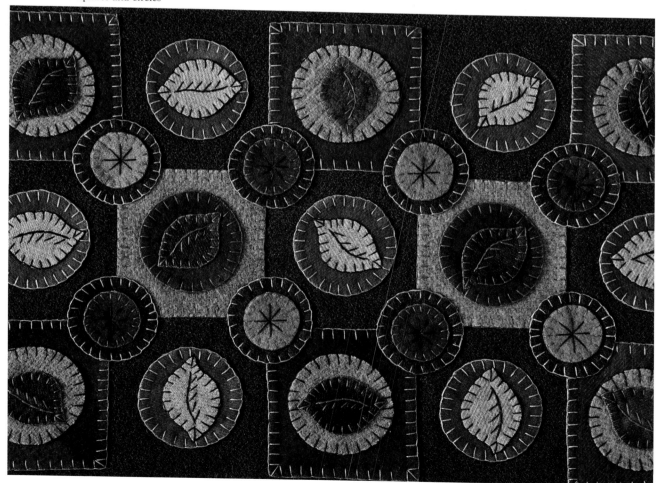

A PATRIOT'S RUG

Finished Rug: 22½″ × 22½″

Americana has long been a favorite style of mine. I love using such iconic motifs as the eagle, shield, flag, stars, and Lady Liberty. These designs were prominently used in the early folk art of America from the time of the revolution to a renewal of patriotic symbols at the 1876 centennial. These images were worked in mediums such as wood, clay, textiles, and iron, to name a few. They represent an important part of our American history.

The eagle is one of the icons I use most often. It's a beautiful and versatile motif for working in wool appliqué. I like the contrast of the curved, flowing eagle with the geometry of the shield and stars. Use this as a striking wallhanging or table rug.

Photo by Garth's Auctioneers & Appraisers, Ohio

This marvelous weather vane illustrates the use of our nation's symbol by an early craftsman.

This is especially nice for those patriotic holidays,
but it also makes a fabulous year-round piece as well.

MATERIALS

Wool

- 1 blue square 22½″ × 22½″ for backing

- 1 dark red square 19½″ × 19½″ for background

- 1 blue rectangle 7″ × 14″ for shields

- 1 red rectangle 10″ × 12″ for shields, eagle bodies, wings, and tails

- 1 black rectangle 6″ × 8″ for circles, half circles, eagle body, and wing accents

- 1 tan rectangle 5″ × 9″ for shields, tails, and heads

- 1 mustard rectangle 4″ × 22″ for stars and starbursts

Other materials

- Embroidery floss: 2 skeins of antique white and 1 skein each of dark brown and dark mustard

GETTING STARTED

Refer to Preparing the Wool Pieces (page 14) as needed for additional details on these steps.

1 Cut out the wool appliqué pieces using the patterns (pullout page P4).

2 Lay out your appliqués according to the pattern to be sure you have all of the pieces.

The eagle is a favorite design motif.

SEWING FUN

Refer to Stitching Your Project (page 14) for details on the blanket stitch and embroidery stitches.

1 Position the eagles, shields, and starbursts on the red background, keeping the pieces within a 17½″ square area as shown. To help with positioning, fold the background in half diagonally in both directions to find the center.

2 Blanket stitch the appliqués in place and embroider the details.

3 Using steam, press the finished piece on the wrong side.

4 Trim the finished piece to 18½″ × 18½″. Refer to Finishing Your Project (page 19) as needed.

5 Center and pin the finished piece to the blue 22½″ backing square. Blanket stitch it to the blue square.

6 Stitch the remaining stars to the backing. Embroider a 5-pointed star inside each.

7 Blanket stitch the outer edges of the backing.

8 Using steam, press the piece on the wrong side.

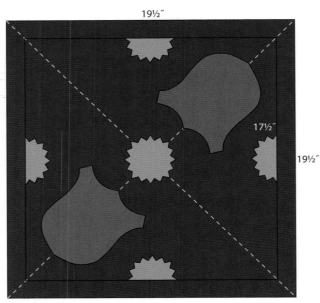

Placement guide

Details of the stitching

The rug in a lighter color combination

SOURCES

WOOL

CROWS ON THE LEDGE

crowsontheledge.com

HEAVENS TO BETSY WOOL

heavens-to-betsy.com

ANTIQUES

GARTH'S AUCTIONEERS & APPRAISERS

garths.com

SPRING STREET ANTIQUES

springstreetantiques.com

HOMESPUN ANTIQUES, KATHY BONNES

440-974-5172

BOOKS ON DYEING WOOL

Primary Fusion Spots with Wool Samples: A Guide to Dyeing Spots & Backgrounds Using Only Three Primaries & Black Pro Chemical Dyes by Ingrid Hieronimus, 1999, Ragg Tyme Studio.

Antique Colors for Primitive Rugs by Emma Lou Lais and Barbara Carroll, 2001, W. Cushing and Company.

SUPPLIES

CHENILLE NEEDLES
Colonial Needle Company • colonialneedle.com

PILLOW FORMS
Fairfield Processing • fairfieldworld.com

FLOSS
DMC • dmc-usa.com

JUTE BAGS
Paper Mart • papermart.com

FREEZER PAPER
C&T Publishing • ctpub.com

ABOUT THE AUTHOR

Antiques have been a part of Rebekah Smith's life from an early age. She grew up surrounded by people who appreciated the simple lines and bold colors of early American folk art. She graduated from the Art Institute of Pittsburgh with a degree in graphic design. It was Rebekah's mother who challenged her to paint in the style of early American muralist Rufus Porter on a cupboard, saying "Try it and you can keep it." Rebekah has never stopped painting on old surfaces. She has studied Rufus Porter's style and Pennsylvania German folk art, both of which continually inspire her work. She also enjoys working on interiors, painting murals, and stenciling.

Her wool work was inspired by a photo of an early American child's bed cover that was appliquéd with animals. Rebekah interpreted this piece into a reality for her youngest daughter. It was her first wool project and resulted in a new, textile-based inspiration. She now repurposes wool and hand dyes it, using a combination of natural and commercial dyes. Rebekah's passion lies in color and design, both talents that are well suited to folk art. She and her husband, along with their three daughters, continually work to restore their 1838 house in the Western Reserve of Ohio.

Visit Rebekah's website at rebekahlsmith.com and her blog at rebekahlsmith.blogspot.com.

Photo by Karly A. Smith

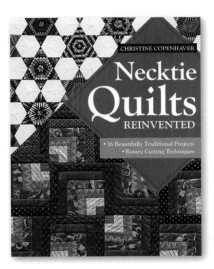
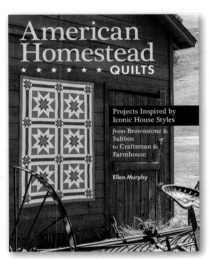
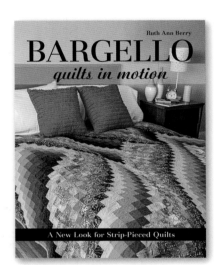
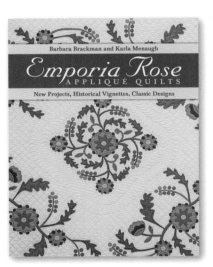